Snake Scales, Barf, and Tails?

Fascinating Snake Facts

Written by Jessica Lee Anderson • Photos by Bob Ferguson II

Paperback ISBN: 978-1-964078-53-3

To Bob, I love working together! Thanks for saying yes and sharing your talents! - JLA

To my son, Wesley - You were my first snake buddy. From getting nipped by watersnakes at two years old to tracking reptiles across foreign landscapes as an adult, you've been in this with me since the very beginning. This journey, and this passion, has always been better with you by my side.- BF

All photos taken by Bob Ferguson II apart from P. 6: Gerasimov174 (skeleton); P. 12: eye-blink (Tiger keelback); P. 15: Ken Griffiths (Yellow-bellied sea snake); P. 23: praisaeng and Mark Kostich (skulls) P. 32: Michael Anderson and Pedro Nahuat

Names of species (current iNaturalist common names) clockwise from top left, unless otherwise noted: Front cover: Rainbow Snake; Title Page: Central American Eyelash-Viper; Dedication: Northern Pine Snake; Copyright: Colorado Desert Shovelnosed snake; P. 4: Yellow Anaconda, Central American Milksnake, Eastern Glass Lizard; P. 5: Small-spotted Cat-eyed Snake, Long-nosed Snake, South American Bushmaster; P. 6: Florida Cottonmouth, Gaboon Viper; P. 7: Crowned False Boa, Hemprich's Coralsnake, Long-nosed Snake; P. 8: Northern Ringneck Snake, Southern Hognose Snake, Eastern Copperhead; P. 9: Eastern "Black" Ratsnake, Osborne's Lancehead, Timber Rattlesnake; P. 10: Eastern Garter Snake, Northern Black Racer, Great Plains Ground Snake; P. 11: Northern Pine Snake, Eastern Copperhead, Eastern Milksnake; P. 12: African Bush Viper, Boomslang, Tiger Keelback; P. 13: Eastern Hognose Snake, Rinkhals, Emerald Tree Boa; P. 14: Speckled Kingsnake, Northern Rubber Boa, Eastern Coralsnake; P. 15: Florida Green Watersnake, Saltmarsh Snake, Green Anaconda, Yellow-bellied sea snake; P. 16: Common Blunt-headed Tree Snake, Green Jararaca, Corn Snake; P. 17: Common Blunt-headed Tree Snake, Green Jararaca, Corn Snake; P. 18: Variable Coralsnake, Osborne's Lancehead, Western Rainbow Boa; P. 19: Asp Viper, Eastern Diamondback Rattlesnake, Western Ribbon Coralsnake; P. 20: Dusky Pygmy Rattlesnake, Gaboon Viper, Eastern Copperhead; P: 21: Southern Pacific Rattlesnake, Northern Cottonmouth, Eastern Hognose Snake; P. 22: Eastern Garter Snake, Everglades Ratsnake (with tick), Northern Pine Snake (snake fungal disease); P. 23: Eastern Kingsnake/Eastern Wormsnake, Graceful Snail-eater, Eastern Ratsnake; P. 24: Eastern Indigo Snake, Western Coachwhip, Smooth Greensnake; P. 25: Smooth Earthsnake, Eastern Milksnake/Northern Redbelly Snake, Eastern Hognose Snake/Spotted Salamander; P. 26: Northern Pine Snake, Northern Black Racer Eggs, Timber Rattlesnakes; P. 27: Northern Pine Snake, Northern Black Racer Eggs, Timber Rattlesnakes; P. 28: Northern Watersnakes, Eastern Milksnakes/Northern Ringneck Snakes, Eastern Copperheads; P. 29: Eastern (Yellow) Ratsnake, South American Bushmaster, Rainbow Snake; P. 30: Northern Redbelly Snakes, Burmese Python, P. 31: Central American Boa, Linnaeus' Sipo, Sonoran Desert Sidewinder, P. 32: Corn Snake, Central American Milksnake (in a cave in the Yucatán Peninsula); Back cover: Yucatán Cantil

This Book Belongs to:

_____

Differences Between Snakes and Legless Lizards

Snake

Almost all snakes have a fixed eye membrane called a spectacle or brille. Brilles protect snake eyes from dirt and other debris.

Snakes are reptiles with long bodies, scales, and no limbs. They are in the same order, or taxonomy rank, as lizards. Some lizards may have no legs and look like snakes, but unlike snakes, legless lizards have eyelids that move, plus visible ear holes.

Legless lizard

Do Snakes Blink?

Without eyelids that move, snakes can't blink. "Shuteye" still happens for snakes even if they can't actually shut their eyes to sleep. Their pupils (the black part of the eye) restrict, meaning less light enters, allowing the snake to rest.

Snakes have tear ducts that keep their eyes moist. Brilles prevent snake eyes from drying out, and they tend to give snake eyes a glassy look.

Bones and Tails

Snakes are not all tails. They have long bodies with short tails in comparison. A snake's tail begins at an opening on the underside called a cloaca.

All reptiles breathe air and have scales instead of fur, hair, or feathers. They are known as vertebrates because they have backbones. Snakes have many ribs and bones called vertebrae (up to 400!) in their flexible backbone.

Scales

Scales vary in size and shape. They are made from keratin, the same protein that forms your skin and hair. Scales protect snakes from injuries, but they also provide traction, allowing snakes to grip to a surface and slither forward. The wide, large scales on a snake's belly are called ventral scales. Scales can vary in texture from smooth to bumpy, and some snakes may have a reduced number of scales.

Many snake species may look slimy, but that's because they have smooth, shiny scales.

Snakeskin

Scales are the hardy outer part of a snake's skin that doesn't expand or stretch the way human skin does. The inner skin layer is called the dermis. Snakes shed their skin throughout their lives to create more room as they grow and age. This process is called ecdysis.

Several species look dry or rough because of keeled scales—a ridge, or keel, runs down the center of the scales.

"In Blue"

Snakes enter a phase that's often called "in blue" before shedding their skin. A second skin layer made of keratin builds on top of the dermis and below the scaly layer. The snake secretes fluid that loosens the old layer of skin from the new one. The fluid can make a snake's eyes appear milky or bluish.

While in blue, snakes can't see as well as usual, so they may be easier to startle or may act more defensively.

"Cold-Blooded"

Like other kinds of reptiles, snakes are "cold-blooded" (though biologists might use more exact terms like ectothermic or poikilothermic). Snakes rely on the environment to stay the right temperature and will often bask in various spots to warm up.

The body temperature of snakes fluctuates—it does not mean their blood stays cold.

Diurnal and Nocturnal

Certain snake species like hognose snakes, king snakes, and pine snakes are diurnal, meaning they are most active during the day. Other snake species like night snakes, certain pythons, and copperheads are nocturnal, or more active at night.

Crepuscular snakes like corn snakes, milk snakes, and certain rattlesnake species are most active at dawn and dusk.

Venom

The majority of snakes are nonvenomous. Many constrict or squeeze their prey. Venomous snakes use venom, a toxic secretion, as a tool for hunting and defense. Venom is made from protein and chemicals, and it ranges in potency from mild to deadly. Researchers have developed human medications from snake venom!

The tiger keelback snake is both venomous AND poisonous (toxic if touched or eaten)!

Snake Teeth

Many snakes have pointed, curved teeth, but they don't use them to chew. Snake teeth grip prey that is then swallowed whole. Venomous snakes have sharp, specialized teeth called fangs they use to inject venom. Venomous snakes may be front-fanged (fangs at the front of the upper jaw) or rear-fanged (fangs towards the back of the upper jaw). Front fangs are either fixed (stay in place) or hinged (fold out like a pocket-knife). Snakes lose and replace teeth throughout their lives!

Rinkhals and certain cobras have the ability to spit venom from short fangs located at the front of their mouth!

13

Families of Snakes

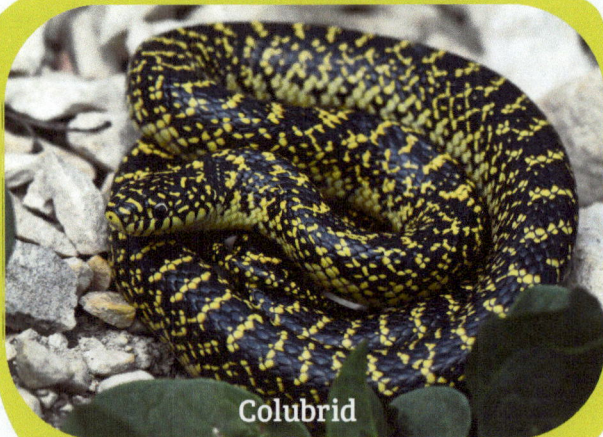
Colubrid

Snakes are organized into groups called families that share similar traits. There are more than 20 snake families! The colubrid family is the largest. Other families include elapids, vipers, boas, pipe snakes, and more.

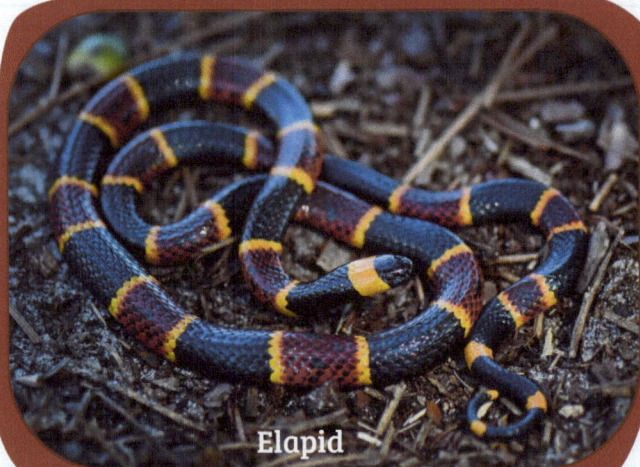
Elapid

Boa

Aquatic

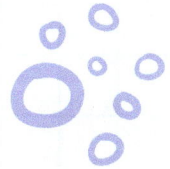

While all snakes can swim, several snake species spend most of their lives around either freshwater or saltwater. Certain species may have flattened heads and/or flat bodies, plus tails that work like paddles.

Arboreal

Arboreal snakes are adapted to living in the trees. These snakes are often thin and agile, making it easier to glide along branches. Some arboreal snakes have prehensile tails that grasp and support their weight when clinging to branches.

Terrestrial and Fossorial

Terrestrial snakes, or land snakes, spend their lives on land in a variety of habitats from grasslands to deserts. Fossorial snakes burrow underground. Many fossorial snakes have heads that are less flexible, and they tend to eat smaller prey (like worms) compared to other species.

Colors

Snakes come in a wide variety of colors from tones of the earth to vibrant greens, yellows, blues, and mixes of different colors. Bright colors serve as a warning to potential predators that the snake may taste disgusting or could cause illness. This is known as aposematism. Certain species have iridescent scales that create a rainbow sheen when light hits them just right.

Patterns

Snakes exhibit many different kinds of patterns like stripes, bands, checkers, chevrons, blotches, spots, and more. Patterns are unique, and there can be variations even in the same species. Just like bright colors, bold patterns can possibly intimidate potential predators. Patterns also serve as a form of communication for some species.

Camouflage

As predators, snakes keep populations of animals like rodents in check, reducing the possible spread of disease. Snakes are also prey for many types of animals such as birds of prey and coyotes. Camouflage adaptations help snakes blend into their environment and go unnoticed by potential predators. Camouflage also makes it easier for snakes to hunt prey.

Defense!

Besides camouflage, snakes have other methods of defense—releasing stinky musk, hissing, mouth gaping, or striking. Rattlesnakes will often rattle a warning, and even nonvenomous snakes will shake their tails. In an attempt to be left alone, a few snake species will fake their own death.

Survival Strategies

In cold climates, certain snakes slow down in a process called brumation that is similar to hibernation, though they still have some activity. Snakes can go months without eating! In harsh climates, some species will collect snow or rain on their scales to drink. Snakes can get fungal and bacterial infections, and they will bask to boost their immune system. If infected with ticks or mites, a snake will soak in water and shed the outer skin.

Super Skulls

Most snake species have flexible heads due to skulls that have mobile joints (kinetic skulls). Snakes don't dislocate their jaws to eat. Instead, they can eat meals larger than their head because their jawbones, or mandibles, are not fused (or stuck) together and are connected by super stretchy ligaments.

Tongues

Snakes have forked tongues that are used to smell instead of taste. Snakes flick their tongues in the air to gather scents that are then detected by the Jacobson's organ. A special tube near a snake's tongue is called the glottis and allows the snake to breathe when swallowing a meal whole. Snakes eat things like insects, rodents, amphibians, other snakes, and more.

Glottis

Barf?

Snakes eliminate waste (pee and poop) from the cloaca. The cloaca is also part of a snake's reproductive system. Snakes might barf, or regurgitate to be more exact, as a form of defense if they become stressed. They may also regurgitate if they get too hot or cold or if they swallow a meal that is too big in order to prevent internal injuries.

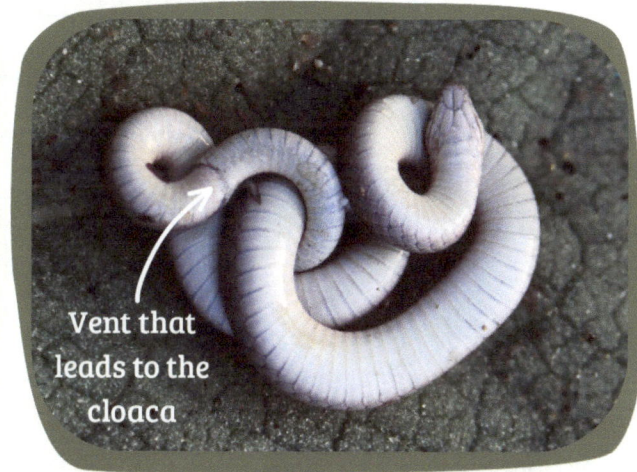

Vent that leads to the cloaca

Regurgitation

Reproduction

Many snakes lay eggs to reproduce (oviparous). Instead of laying eggs, other species give live birth (viviparous) or will retain the eggs inside of their body until they are ready to hatch (ovoviviparous).

Hearing and Vision

Snakes may lack external ear openings, but they can still hear (even if it is different than the way you hear sounds). Most snakes have good vision, though some fossorial snakes like blind snakes have reduced eyes or no eyes at all. Pit vipers and many boas and pythons have heat pits that work like night-vision goggles to search for prey.

Social Groups

While a number of snake species live alone, others den together in the winter or gather during times of courtship. Researchers have observed how various snakes seem to prefer the company of specific snakes while avoiding others.

Snake Safety

Snakes don't hunt people and prefer to be left alone. To avoid a conflict with a snake, stay on trails when you spend time outdoors, wear appropriate footwear, and watch where you step (especially in the dark). Also, avoid reaching into places you can't see.

From Mini to Massive

There are around 4,000 species of snakes in the world! They vary in size and weight depending on the species. Some are shorter than a smartphone and thinner than a pencil while others can grow to be as long as a school bus and as heavy as some motorcycles.

Spectacular Snakes

Snakes exist on every continent except Antarctica. The highest number of snake species can be found in Mexico.

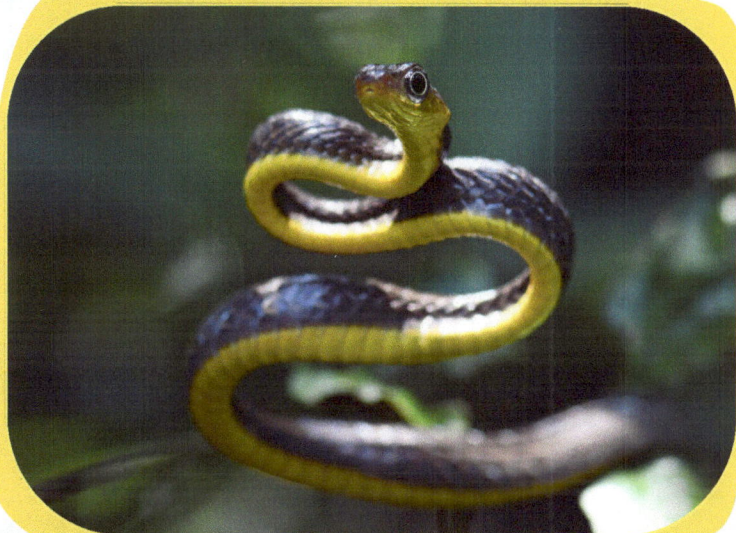

Scientists are continuing to learn more about snakes and snake venom. New snake species are still being discovered! Snakes are essential for healthy ecosystems.

Jessica Lee Anderson is an award-winning author of over 100 books for young readers including the NAOMI NASH chapter book series. Jessica loves spending time in nature and exploring the outdoors with her husband, Michael, and their daughter, Ava! Jessica volunteers to relocate snakes caught in tricky situations and has a corn snake named Ari. You can learn more about Jessica by visiting www.jessicaleeanderson.com.

Bob is a naturalist with a compulsion to be outdoors. Wildlife conservation through entertainment, education, fundraising, and fieldwork is his mission and purpose in life. His organization, Fascinature, has donated six figures to saving land in the world's most biodiverse spaces. He even has a frog named after him! You can find him on Instagram @bob_ferguson_fascinature or sign up for his newsletter at fascinature.live.

Check out these other books!

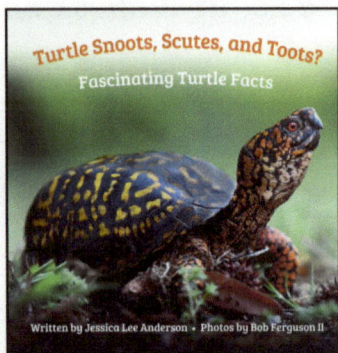

Turtle Snoots, Scutes, and Toots?
Fascinating Turtle Facts

Written by Jessica Lee Anderson • Photos by Bob Ferguson II

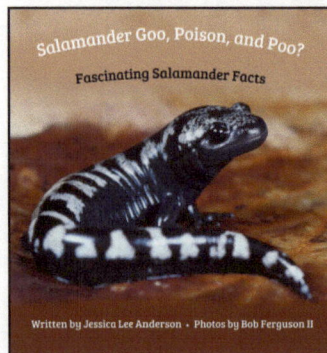

Salamander Goo, Poison, and Poo?
Fascinating Salamander Facts

Written by Jessica Lee Anderson • Photos by Bob Ferguson II

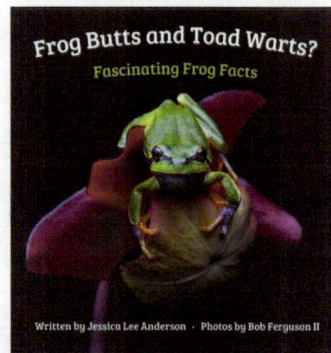

Frog Butts and Toad Warts?
Fascinating Frog Facts

Written by Jessica Lee Anderson • Photos by Bob Ferguson II